DAILY MIRROR, Monday, October 23, 1939

DAILY Mirror

No. 11,194   ♦ ♦   ONE PENNY
Registered at the G.P.O. as a Newspaper

BRITAIN WINS FIRST WEEK OF AIR WAR

14 Nazi Bombers Shot Down in 6 Days

EVERY ENEMY AIR RAID ON THE BRITISH COAST HAS BEEN DRIVEN OFF WITH HEAVY LOSS TO THE GERMANS. ANOTHER NAZI BOMBER — THE FOURTEENTH IN SIX DAYS—WAS SHOT DOWN YESTERDAY IN THE SEA OFF THE EAST COAST OF SCOTLAND.

As sirens shrieked a warning to towns along the Scottish coast two German machines appeared.

At once British fighters went up. There was a furious battle in the sky. In a few minutes one raider was down.

A collapsible rubber boat was seen to leave the wreck.

And as British planes repulsed the latest attempt to raid our shores ships of the first British convoy to be attacked from the air arrived in port, with seamen who had a tale to tell.

They told of two different attacks at a convoy spread out to form a large target for bombers. Both attacks failed miserably.

Gunfire from the ships and the furious attack of our fighting planes, summoned quickly to the scene, brought down four Nazi raiders. The rest ran for home.

One of the eye-witnesses said: "Three planes dived on us from one side and two from another. Before you could say Jack Robinson the guns of the escorting ships started to rattle.

'Not one bomb was dropped. I think the Nazis were scared with the reception they got.

" Within seconds, it seemed, British fighters were above us chasing off the enemy

"I saw one of the Nazi planes caught by shell fire. It just fluttered its wings and dropped into the sea."

Nazis Poor Shooting

Another said: "I went to the gun station. I had the enemy planes sighted lovely. I say I could have blown them out of the sky

"We asked could we fire, but were not allowed

"If I had been at the breech instead of the sights I don't think I could have resisted

"A vessel to the rear of us let fire as the bombers dived over us

"Talk about the pictures. It was the most exciting thing I have ever seen, but if I had been the gunner of a German plane and I could not do better than he did—well, I'd eat my hat, and I only had a fortnight's course."

Two hours later the enemy planes returned to the attack on the convoy This time only one bomb was seen to drop

"A Direct Hit"

"It dropped only one bomb," the same sailor went on.

"It landed not far from a warship I think and then—bang, the plane had caught a direct hit from one of the warship's guns.

'Our fighters were over us like lightning think they must have scared the Nazi pilots."

A member of another crew in the convoy said: "The warship escorting us gave the Nazi planes ten minutes of hell

"They must have been scared stiff, but in two raids, only one bomb dropped—and it was the last that plane ever dropped."

"It was just an incident in our work," a member of another crew said.

"As a matter of fact, I had been asleep and just went on deck out of curiosity.

"If it is the best the Nazis can do to stop our convoys then we have no need to worry" Mr. Kenneth Luke, chief officer of one ship in the convoy, said:—

"At 12.30 p.m three German bombers appeared to the east flying very high and they dived down over the escort ships which immediately opened anti-aircraft fire.

"I saw one of the German machines lurch

Continued on Back Page

If I Go —Hitler Warns

HITLER conferred all day yesterday with the Nazi State Governors and Party leaders he had summoned to Berlin from all over Germany.

German officials in Berlin describe the meeting as "a conference of historic importance," and it is certain that Hitler was forced to reveal his desperate military and economic position.

For the British and French pact with Turkey has been a major blow to Germany. It strengthens the appeal of the Ribbentrop group who urge Hitler to secure Russia's active help "at any price."

There is no doubt that when the party leaders met yesterday, Hitler sounded them on the probable public reaction to a more pronounced pro-Moscow policy, and the general effect of war on the public morale.

It is known, too, that Hitler took care to share the responsibilities of the war.

"Stick Together" Plea

He told his party chiefs that the Allies seek an end of Hitlerism—and the death of Nazism meant the end of their careers. This warning that "if I go you go" was followed by an appeal to stick together in the hour of fate.

Hitler has already addressed his Army chiefs in the same vein warning them the end of the Nazi regime, through an allied victory, will be the end of the German army too

In his discussions with his naval and military leaders and the ambassadors from Turkey Russia and Italy, Hitler has given his assurance that he will do all he can to get the active help of Moscow and Rome without committing himself too far

But the Fuehrer had to admit that his attempt even to bring Moscow and Rome into a joint consultation has dismally failed.

NEW SOVIET-NAZI MOVES

A NEW and extensive trade agreement between Germany and Russia is expected to be signed in the next few days.

The Soviet Union will buy from Germany considerable equipment for the Soviet Navy and the mercantile marine.

This was reported last night after a Moscow announcement that a Soviet trade mission, headed by P. P. Tevosyan, Commissar for the shipbuilding industry, will leave for Berlin in the near future to supervise the transport of German exports to the U.S.S.R.

Herr Ritter, a special member of the German trade delegation in Moscow, left for Berlin yesterday by plane after the completion of the first stage in the Soviet-German trade negotiations.

A joint communique said the talks have been "proceeding favourably, according to expectations."

From General to Private

General Clement de Grancourt, whose last command in the French Army was over a brigade in Syria, has just rejoined the Colours as a private for the duration of the war.

NICE RAVING, DR. GOEBBELS

DR. Goebbels, Germany's Propaganda Minister, excelled himself last night in the maddest and wildest speech of his career.

He devoted himself wholly to an attack on Mr. Churchill. To listeners he seemed to "froth at the mouth" in his anger.

"We shall get you one day and force you to answer our questions," he screamed almost hysterically.

"None of your lies can make us silent," Goebbels shouted. "Don't pose to be a decent gentleman. Give an answer. A neutral witness, Henderson, gave clear proof that you ordered the sinking of the Athenia by three British destroyers

[Unfortunately the "neutral witness" happens to have the typically German name of Gustav.]

"And now my questions! How dared you to speak in your first conference thus:— Athenia was sunk by a German torpedo when you the First Lord of the British Admiralty knew that three British destroyers had sunk her.

"Where have you, Mr. Churchill, found these criminal witnesses.

"We know we can't expect to hear the truth from you, Mr. Churchill. This would be against your character and your nature and besides this truth would be the death sentence of your political career and therefore let me help you a bit, Mr. Churchill.

Goebbels then gave his "detailed account" of the sinking of the Athenia

"You took care," he shouted, "that American citizens should he on the Athenia because you wanted to have American victims of your crime.

"Acused Winston Churchill, First Lord of the Admiralty, it's up to you now."

CONGRATULATIONS, DR. GOEBBELS— A MAGNIFICENT EFFORT. THE ONLY THING THAT PUZZLES AMERICA NOW IS WHY NONE OF HER MANY CITIZENS ON BOARD SAW THE DESTROYERS. PERHAPS THEY ON THE OTHER SIDE OF THE SHIP WERE. YES?

First published in Great Britain by
Franklin Watts Limited
96 Leonard Street
London EC2 4RH

Franklin Watts Australia
14 Mars Road
Lane Cove
N.S.W. 2066

Franklin Watts Inc
387 Park Avenue South
New York, NY 10016

ISBN: 0 86313 873 X

Design: David Bennett
Editor: Jenny Wood
Picture research: Sarah Ridley
Typeset by Admirable Typesetting, St Albans
Printed in Belgium

Acknowledgements

The author and publisher would like to thank Charlie
and Marion Jones without whom this book would not have been
possible. Thanks also to The Moths and Mothw of the General
Browning Club, Hackney Archive, and The Museum of
the Order of Saint John.

Photographs: Cadbury Ltd 30B; Greater London
Record Office 37T; Hackney Archives 10T, 11B, 16B, 19BL,
42-43; Hulton Deutsch 14BR, 17T, 20B, 21T, 24B, 25B, 26BR,
29T, 29C, 31B, 40TR, 41TL, 41BR, 41BL; Imperial War Museum
14T, 19T, 22, 23BL, 26BL, 30T; Charlie and Marion Jones 8, 12T,
13T, 13B, 14BL, 15, 16T, 32T, 35T, 38B; Leeds Central Library
34B; Museum of East Anglian Life 26T; Popperfoto 10BL, 17B,
18, 20T, 21BR, 28B, 34T, 35B, 40BL, 40BR, 40TL, 41BR;
Syndication International 41TR; Neil Thomson cover, title verso,
10BR, 11T, 12B, 19BR, 21BL, 24T, 25T, 27T, 28C, 29BR, 32B,
36T, 37B, 39, 43R; Vintage Magazine Company 28T.

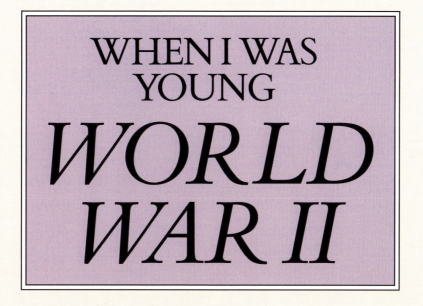

WHEN I WAS YOUNG
WORLD WAR II

NEIL THOMSON
MEETS
CHARLIE JONES

FRANKLIN WATTS
LONDON   NEW YORK   SYDNEY   TORONTO

Charlie Jones lives in north London a few miles from where he was born in 1933. Like many thousands of wartime children he was evacuated to the country to be protected from the German bombing. He returned to London during the war and spent the rest of his childhood there.

After leaving school Charlie served as an apprentice plumber and started work for a local firm building council flats in Hackney. When he was twenty Charlie did his National Service in the army and was posted to Egypt and Libya.

Charlie was married in 1958, he and his wife Marion have three children who still live nearby. Charlie now works in the District Surveyor's Department of Hackney Council.

CONTENTS

Family life in wartime

Me and my family

My name is Charlie Jones. I was born in London in 1933. I had three sisters, called Amy, Ada and Emmy, and one brother, called Fred. I was the youngest in my family by eleven years so, by the time I went to school, my brother and sisters were all working.

When I was six the Second World War started. My dad had been in the army in the First World War, so he was too old to be asked to fight again. I was lucky, I had mum and dad at home. I knew one or two kids whose dad didn't come back from the war.

My dad had a short fuse, he'd fly off the handle very easily. He'd been deafened in the war so he couldn't always hear exactly what was said. He and mum used to argue but they never came to blows — although that did happen in our street!

My mum Ada and my dad Fred. Nobody got muddled even though there were so many people in my family with the same name.

My brother Fred and two of my sisters, Emmy and Ada.

Me at about four years old.

Daily Herald

No. 7349   MONDAY, SEPTEMBER 4, 1939   ONE PENNY

WAR DECLARED BY BRITAIN AND FRANCE

The Fleet Moves Into Position

GREAT BRITAIN DECLARED WAR ON GERMANY AT 11 O'CLOCK YESTERDAY MORNING.

Six hours later, at 5 p.m., France declared war.

Britain's resolution to defend Poland against Na... was described by the newly-formed Ministry of I... one of its first announcements, as follows:—

"At 11.15 this morning (Sunday) Mr. R. Dunbar, Head of the Treaty Department of the Foreign Office, went to the German Embassy, where he was received by Dr. Kordt, the Charge d'Affaires.

"Mr. Dunbar handed to Dr. Kordt a notification that a state of war existed between Great Britain and Germany as from 11 o'clock B.S.T. this morning. This notification constituted the formal declaration of war."

Navy Fully Mobilised

The King broadcast to the nation last night. A copy of his message, with facsimile signature, will be distributed to every household in the country.

Britain's Navy is fully mobilised and is at its war stations in full strength, supplemented by a number of fully commissioned armed merchant ships as auxiliary cruisers.

The convoy system for merchant shipping has been introduced.

The King has made the following appointments: Commander-in-Chief of the British Field Forces, General Viscount Gort, V.C.; Chief of the Imperial General Staff, General Sir Edmund Ironside; Commander-in-Chief of the Home Forces, General Sir Walter Kirke.

The Empire has sprung to Britain's support, "Australia is at war," declared Mr. Menzies, the Commonwealth Prime Minister, broadcasting last night.

"Where Britain stands," he said, "there stands the people of the Empire and the British world."

"All Possible Support"

The New Zealand Government has sent a tele... 'immediately associating" itself with the British Go... ment. "All possible support" is assured.

The Viceroy of India has issued a proclam... announcing the outbreak of war.

It is understood that the Japanese Governm... given the British Government assurances of ... neutrality.

Hitler left Berlin last night for the Polish Fron... he is to assume command of the German armies.

Sir Nevile Henderson, the British Ambassador, ... Coulondre, the French Ambassador, took their ... Herr von Ribbentrop, German Foreign Minister, ... Neither envoy saw Hitler.

To-day has been declared a Bank Holiday, ... only banks and does not apply to any other bu... banks will reopen to-morrow.—Details on Pag...

Petrol is to be controlled and rati... September 16. One grade only will be supp... be called "Pool Motor Spirit," and will cost 1s...

All cinemas, theatres and other places of ... are closed until further notice.

Premier Sees King

The Prime Minister, who, in a broadcast to the nation, had declared: "We have resolved to finish it," visited the King at Buckingham Palace last night. War Minister Hore-Belisha also saw the King.

Mr. Arthur Greenwood, Acting Leader of the Opposition, in a broadcast, said: "If we do not overthrow the forces of dictatorship now, our turn will come sooner or later."

Unthinkable We Should Refuse The Challenge

—THE KING

Broadcasting last evening from his study at Buckingham Palace, the King said:—

POLES SMASH WAY INTO E. PRUSSIA

OFFICIALS in Warsaw stated late last night that the Polish army has smashed a way across the Northern border into East Prussia, after driving the Germans from several Polish towns in bitter fighting.

London Hears Its First Raid Warning

...eard its first air raid
...the Air Ministry:—

ACK-OUT TIME NIGHT—7.40

On the Northern Front the Poles are reported to have defeated the German effort to drive a barrier across the upper part of the Corridor. The Germans fell back behind their frontiers.

The Poles say they have broken through the German fortifications as far as the railway terminus of Deutsch Eylau.

One of the most important towns recaptured is stated to be Zbaszyn. Early to-day an official Polish communiqué admitted, however, that Polish troops had been compelled to abandon Czestochowa, about 37 miles from frontier of Upper Silesia.

(Continued on Page 2; Earlier fighting details on Page 10)

Identity cards were introduced in September 1939. Even children had to have them.

prevail. May He bless and ... all.

... large centres (Reuter says).

9

"It never hits the same house twice"

We lived in Stoke Newington in north London. My parents had lived in the area since they were kids. In 1939, when the war started, we lived in Cowper Road — we didn't have a garden then, just a concrete back yard.

In 1940, when a house round the corner in Spenser Grove came empty, we moved in there. We didn't have much furniture. We just put everything in a wheelbarrow and round we went. The house had been bomb-blasted before we moved, but my mum said, "We'll be all right here, it never hits the same house twice." She was right, too — only one house in our street was destroyed in the blitz.

Houses in Spenser Grove. They were demolished by the council in the 1960s and the flats below were built in their place.

Families often had to move when their homes were hit. By May 1941 almost one-and-a-half million people in London had been made homeless.

"You were cissy if you had carpet"

We had electricity for the first time in the new house, but no gas. In Cowper Road, where we lived before, we had gas for lighting. People kept the gas mantles just in case there was no electricity or they didn't have a shilling for the meter.

There was a fireplace in every room but we never lit a fire in the bedrooms unless someone was ill and in bed. I used to go round the corner to the coal merchants and bring back a wheelbarrowful for the kitchen stove.

There was no carpet in the house, just a small bit in front of the fire. People would have thought you were cissy if you had carpet. We just had oilcloth on the floors.

Some of the houses in our street had two or three families living in them, so we were quite well off with a house to ourselves.

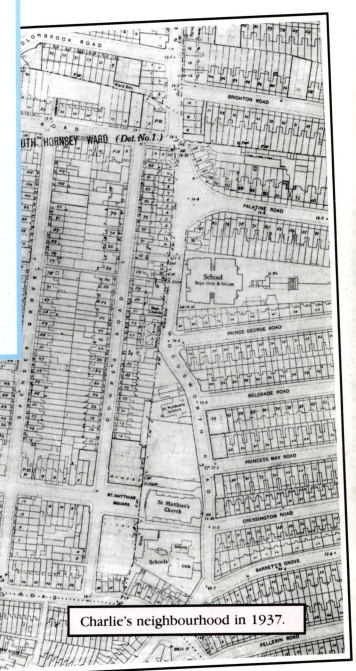

Charlie's neighbourhood in 1937.

"The laundry was like a club"

The new house was on three floors. There was no bathroom, just a sink with a cold tap on the landing. The toilet was outside in the garden. When we wanted hot water we had to heat up a kettle on the stove in the kitchen. We went round to the public baths in Milton Grove to have a proper hot bath. There was a laundry there as well. Mum went there on Saturdays, it was like a club. I'd go round there about 4 o'clock with a pram and help her bring the washing home.

In the whole road at that time there were only three or four cars. There were plenty of horses, though, and we used to nip out with a shovel to pick up the manure for the garden. Even now, when I see a horse in the street I look round for a shovel and think, "Ooh, that'd be great on the rhubarb."

My mum knitting clothes for her grandchildren.

The public laundry in Milton Grove, rebuilt since the war and now closed.

At home normal life carried on as much as possible. Adverts usually ignored the war.

ORE WASHING I'LL GO MAD SOON!

"GLORY – HOW CAN I EVER KEEP YOU KIDS CLEAN? I CAN'T EVEN AFFORD ALL THE SOAPS AND THINGS I NEED FOR MY WASH AS IT IS."

"TUT, TUT! DON'T SCOLD THE KIDDIES. IF YOU USED OXYDOL YOU'D DO YOUR WASH FOR ABOUT HALF THE MONEY AND GET EVERYTHING CLEANER AND BRIGHTER, TOO!"

In the back room on the ground floor was dad's workshop. He was a locksmith, but there wasn't much call for him around our street. Most people left the front door unlocked or kept the key hanging on a string inside the letter box. Anyway, there wasn't much to pinch, only the wireless. It was a great big thing, larger than a telly is now.

Dad used to sharpen knives and saws as well as being a locksmith. It was a bit noisy, I don't know how the neighbours put up with it, but since dad was so deaf the noise didn't bother him much.

He used to threaten me with the belt for messing around with his tools. Once I sharpened my pencil on his razor and made it blunt. When he went to shave, he was furious. He said it was like shaving with a saw.

My mum was out at work most of the time. She worked in a clothing factory nearby, making men's suits. She used to bring home jackets to work on. I sometimes helped her take out the stitches and got a penny for every jacket I did.

My dad with some of the kids from our street.

Evacuation

"They wanted to adopt me"

I'd only just started school when the war began and the Government decided to send all the children out of London to escape the bombing. My school, Princess May, was officially evacuated to Letchworth, in Hertfordshire.

It was the first time I'd ever been on a train and it felt exciting, like going on a holiday. Most of us had never been out of London before. I think the parents worried more than the kids. The day after I had been sent away, my brother Fred cycled out to Letchworth to see that I was all right. I stayed with an oldish lady and her husband. They wanted to adopt me, but my mum said she wanted me back, so I wasn't there long.

In the first week of September 1939 almost one-and-a-half million people left the cities in the official evacuation. Most children left without their parents.

Me in Letchworth, I think we'd been to a wedding.

The train journey was often slow and always crowded. Children wore labels to identify them.

GOVERNMENT EVACUATION SCHEME.
METROPOLITAN EVACUATING AREA.

Application for Cheap Railway Facilities for Visits.

BEFORE FILLING IN THIS FORM PLEASE STUDY THE INFORMATION
GIVEN ON THE BACK.

Section 1. **To be completed by the applicant.**

I declare that the cheap t~~~~~~~~~ facilities for which I am applying are for the
purpose of visiting the underm~~~~~~~~~~~~~~~~~~~~~~~~~~~~ho have been
evacuated from _Stoke New~~~_

I further declare that I have boo~~~~~~~~~~~~~~~~~~~~~~~~~~~
be away on a visit.

Address _95 Cowper Roa~_
~~~~~ New~~g~

Me and my sister with her daughter in Scotland.

I got sent to a convent school in Letchworth, where they made you eat up all your food. I had tapioca and it was so horrible seeing it for the first time I just couldn't eat it. I was taken in front of the Mother Superior and got a real telling-off. It was frightening — I'd never seen nuns before.

After a few months, mum came to get me and we went to Scotland to stay with my sister who was living there. I was the only English boy in my class, but there were a couple of kids who looked after me, so I was never in any bother. I remember once the teacher was talking about some battle the Scots had lost and all the kids looked round at me as though it was all my fault. They used to call me *the little Sassenach.*

~~~~~~ and ~~~~

~mature~ _____

Qualification _____ _Councillor_

"We listened to the wireless every day"

I kept moving around at the beginning of the war. I had more time off school than at school and it felt like a long holiday. After Scotland, I went to stay near Oxford. My sister, Ada, made the arrangements. Her husband, Sid, was in the ARP. He used to help make sure people were in a shelter during the air raids. He was sent to Oxford for a rest period and stayed in this big farmhouse. When he came home, Ada wrote to the family and asked if we could go there.

The family was quite well off. They had two cars. One was on blocks in the garage but they had petrol for the other one. I think they were given an allowance because the lady was disabled. I used to work on the farm, going round with the tractor in the corn stooks.

Me and my brother-in-law Sid.

The ARP wardens were local men and women. After bombing raids they helped the fire brigade and the ambulance service look for survivors.

Hitler's Plan For Britain

By
MADAME TABOUIS

● HITLER, on June 4, informed his staff and his colleagues of his plans for the coming months.

● After reminding them that he would be in Paris on June 15, as he had arranged with Göring, Goebbels, and Himmler, he declared that he would not give Britain time to organise herself, that he would attack her round about July 2, according to the plan previously arranged.

● Therefore, he explained, France must be put out of any state capable of resisting, at least on t̶h̶e̶ ̶ an Conti-

Petrol was rationed to conserve supplies for essential journeys.

uday Disp

JUNE 23, 1940.

POSTAGE IN U.K.
AND NEWFOUNDLAI
OTHER PLACES A

CH SIGN ARMIST

overnment's Grie

NAZI

ll Appeals To
en: 'Fight On'

PLENIPOTENTIARIES SIGNED
VITH GERMANY AT 5.30 LAST
PIEGNE, FRANCE, WHERE THE
E WAS SIGNED

ill not take effect until six hours after a
an agreement has been reached," stated
which added that the French pleni-
pected to arrive at the appointed meeting
y.

out the terms of the armistice were known last

Ally"

rnment have heard with grief and amazement that
he Germans have

Once the lady said I could earn some money picking lavender for her to make little bags with. I earned £4, which was a lot of money then, and I bought a toy glider which I flew in the garden. We used to make toys: soap-box type carts with wheels with ball-bearings, spinning tops and tanks made out of cotton reels and a piece of candle. We played marbles in the street. I used to play right along the gutter all the way to school. It used to take ages sometimes to get to school like that.

While we were in Oxford, we had a map of Europe with cut-out flags to show where the armies were. We listened to the wireless every day and as soon as we heard that the flying bombs had stopped, we went back to London.

ors

oe

CRACK GE
BEEN TORPE
M, NORWAY
DAMAGE."
stroyer was

rs and screen
hters, Scharn
s she slunk ou
ay to a port
y a heavy Br

ing, scored a

s, informed
d the Nazi s

LATEST

PRISONERS
New list of B
roadcast on Ge
night:
Pilot Officer
Flying Officer
ng Aircraftm
kenzie, Pilot
Whiting, Pilot
Farhurst, Pil
Stapleton, Fly
Bretherton,
Oliver, Pilot
James, Serge
Pilot Officer
ster, Sergea
Richard Whi
Glasgow; H
forth, near

"SUB"

craft failed to return.
Scharnhorst, launched only in
January of last year, ran away,
dly damaged, when attacked
the Renown in N

Radios were essential for both information and entertainment. Television broadcasts did not start until after the war.

17

Bombing and shelters

"No sleep at all"

London was still being bombed after we came back from Oxford, but people had almost got used to it. When you heard the siren, you just got up and ran to the shelter. Sometimes the sirens went on all night and you got no sleep at all. When there was an air raid, we used to put cotton wool in our ears and a rubber between our teeth — so even if we'd been killed, we wouldn't have been deafened.

You could hear the doodlebugs. They were worse than the rockets, which were completely silent. You never knew what would get hit. There was a big bang one night, and the next morning the school down the road had gone completely. Luckily it was empty, so I don't think anyone was killed. After that all the kids from there came to our school. We thought it was great because we only had half days then so they could fit in all the new kids.

Daylight bombing raids caused many casualties. In the first two years of the war as many civilians as soldiers were killed.

Many homes were destroyed by the German bombing raids. When the bombs exploded, they flattened the buildings they hit and the blast could damage buildings several streets away.

Saint Mathias church after bomb damage.

Shakespeare Road just behind us was bombed, completely flattened. The church round the corner, Saint Mathias, was hit too. It was a great area to play on afterwards. But we used to play on the streets — there were no cars in the way then.

We went down to south London to see an auntie one night during the blitz. There was a big raid, with enormous guns going off and great searchlights. It was like a big fireworks display. My mum said, "You'd better come and look at this because your grandchildren are going to be paying for the damage." The next day, you could see houses with the baths all hanging out of the walls and all the pipes showing.

My auntie's son was killed later on in the war. He was in the navy and died on the battleship HMS Hood. He was the only one in our family who was killed, though. My brother Fred served in both the army and the navy but he never left the country. We were lucky, really.

Saint Mathias church now.

"There were spiders and everything"

We had an Anderson shelter in the garden but it was too horrible to use, it was so wet and damp and cold. Some people had a hand pump to keep their shelter dry, but I don't remember ever sleeping in ours — there were spiders and everything. Anyway, we reckoned if a bomb did hit our house then the shelter would probably go as well.

If we were caught out of doors in a raid, we'd go down the shelter in Allen Road underneath the Post Office. There'd be thirty or forty people down there, sitting on benches. We used to go down the big shelter under the flats in Howard Road. I don't think we were officially allowed in, but we pretended we lived there.

The shelters became social clubs. They used to have shows with everyone singing songs. Old music-hall songs were the favourites. Most nights someone would play the accordion or do magic tricks and there was a canteen as well.

Anderson shelters, named after their designer, being delivered in north London in 1939.

Thousands of people took shelter in the London Underground. Concerts were put on to take people's minds off the war.

Cinemas and theatres were closed for the first three months of the war. Audiences were not put off going out for the evening when they reopened.

Allen Road Post Office now.

Gas masks and blackouts

DAILY EXPRESS. Tuesday, August 13, 1940.

Lovely Lasting **BEAR BRAND** PURE SILK STOCKINGS

BLACK-OUT ZERO HOUR TO-NIGHT UNTIL 5.15 A.M. MOON RISES 5.17 P.M. MOON SETS 2.13 A.M.

No. 12,550

Daily G

Tuesday, August

The Battle of Britain is on: Hitler

Newspapers printed the times for the blackout every day.

"You were always saying sorry"

Everybody had to put up the blackouts every night so that the German bombers couldn't see any lights showing. We had a frame covered with black cloth for each window. The ARP wardens and the police used to check to make sure there wasn't even a chink of light.

In the winter, in the blackout, it was really dark — even on the main road. Sometimes you were out and you'd see a big flash, and you'd know there'd been a rocket. But on the High Street it could have been a trolleybus — they used to make a big spark. Torch batteries were difficult to find, so a torch was very precious. We sometimes went around with our shirt tails hanging out so we'd be easier to see.

It was difficult walking around in the blackout. You were always saying sorry after you'd bumped into something and then you'd realise it was a lamp-post.

The ARP wardens carried lamps or torches in case they needed to look for casualties. One-and-a-half million people joined the Civil Defence Force.

We all had to have a gas mask, because people were frightened the Germans might use poison gas. I was always worried I might lose my mask. It was kept in a box, but that was more useful for keeping other things in.

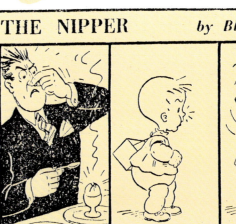

THE NIPPER *by* BRIAN WHITE

Even babies had to have a helmet to protect against possible gas attack.

Hitler will send no warning –

so always carry your gas mask

ISSUED BY THE MINISTRY OF HOME SECURITY

The government produced leaflets to help people at home prepare for the war.

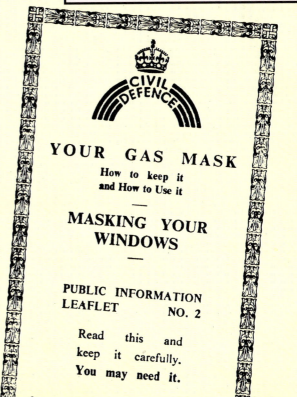

CIVIL DEFENCE

YOUR GAS MASK

How to keep it and How to Use it

—

MASKING YOUR WINDOWS

—

PUBLIC INFORMATION LEAFLET   NO. 2

Read this and keep it carefully. **You may need it.**

School

"Boys had to have very short hair"

We didn't talk much about the war in school. In the morning assembly, the head would say if a battle had been won, but we didn't really understand.

There were only boys in my class, about thirty-five or forty of us, the girls were in separate classes. We couldn't wear long trousers until our last year. The boys had to have very short hair or we'd be threatened with the cane, or even have our hair tied up in ribbons.

Many schools had separate entrances for boys and girls.

Charlie's primary school was damaged in the blitz. It is still in use now.

Teachers made sure children had their gas masks. The masks were never needed. The Germans never used poison gas in the bombing raids on London.

"Nittie Nora, the nit explorer"

The school nurse used to come round checking for head lice. The kids called her Nittie Nora, the nit explorer. We took a mug to school every day to get milk, and we were given cod liver oil and malt as well.

The teacher was very strict. He used to rap my knuckles with a ruler for not spelling properly, and he'd throw chalk at us if we were talking in class. All you had to do was answer back and you'd get the cane. Some of the boys got caned a lot. They liked to be tough and say it didn't hurt, but it must have done.

When I got my bike, I came home down a short cut, an alleyway called Town Hall Approach. You weren't meant to ride your bike down there, so if you saw a copper you jumped off quick. If you had no lights on your bike at night and they spotted you, you thought you'd get sent to a reform school. Of course, in the war, you had to put a cover over your bicycle lamp for the blackout.

Rationing

"A fraction of a banana"

A lot of things were more difficult to get in the war. There were ration books, and coupons for things like butter. It was the first time a lot of people in Stoke Newington had ever had butter when they had the coupons. Before the war they had margarine or dripping. Mum had a green ration book to get luxuries like oranges or chocolate.

My brother-in-law, Harry, was in Gibraltar at the end of the war and he used to send us food parcels. They were for my sister, Emmy, really, but we all used to share. It was quite something to get a parcel. We got one grape each and a fraction of a banana all cut up. We got a pickled banana once! It was horrible, and I'd always thought bananas were meant to be nice.

The government published recipes to help people cook unfamiliar foods.

RECIPES FOR Salt Fish

During the next three months, we shall have less than half the fresh fish which we had in the summer, and catches will not improve until the early spring.

To help make up for the loss of fresh fish, Canada and Newfoundland are sending us extra supplies, mainly of cod. To keep it in condition during its long journey the fish is heavily salted and it is necessary to remove this salt by soaking in water for about 24 hours. But remember that once the salt is out, the fish must be treated like fresh cod and cooked the same day. The price is 10d. per lb.

Don't go at it slap-dash. Give it a little time and attention, try new dishes with it and you will find this fish very good to eat as well as cheap and a change. Here are some suggestions to start with.

DIG FOR VICTORY

The government's Dig For Victory campaign meant vegetables did not have to be rationed.

Allotments at the Tower of London.

My dad had an allotment in Clissold Park which had been all dug up so people could grow food. I used to help him there with the digging. We had chickens and rabbits as well. We got an allowance for their feed, but then we weren't allowed an egg ration. Of course, on the allotment, everything came at once, so we gave a lot away. Nobody had a fridge then.

We didn't eat too badly in the war. Breakfast was bread and marge, bread and sugar if we were really lucky, and toast if the fire happened to be lit. We didn't have a toaster, you just held a bit of bread on a toasting fork in front of the fire. We got bread from the baker's van or horse and cart. It was always white. Brown bread would have been something foreign, something the Germans would have had.

RATIONS
The answers to your questions

? How big a ham sandwich can I get for half a bacon coupon? —A sandwich containing two ounces of ham.

? Can I order bread and butter or a roll and butter in a restaurant without giving up a coupon?—Yes.

? Can I get butter without a coupon at a staff canteen?— Yes, at all catering establishments.

? Are fried eggs and bacon or fried eggs and ham exempt?— No, you must give up a coupon for them if you order them in a restaurant.

? If bacon and ham are rationed, what about pork?—Pork is not rationed. Nor are pork sausages, pigs' trotters, liver, kidneys, chitterlings, and other offals.

? If I live in London, my wife and family (evacuated) in, say, Exeter, do we register with two grocers, and what

C.M.S.3

TO BE RETAINED
BY THE
HOUSEHOLDER

MINISTRY OF FOOD
PERMIT FOR THE SUPPLY OF MILK
AT·TWO PENCE PER PINT

P 545

Name and Address of householder: *Frederick H. White. 105 Casimir Rd*

is authorised to obtain on the condition given overleaf the quantity of milk mentioned below milk retailer of his or her choice.

Date **10 OCT 1941**

form of application for the renewal of this permit obtainable from the MILK OFFICER HACKNEY ust be submitted at least fourteen days before the new Permit is required. case of temporary absence from home see note 3 overleaf.

First

"A halfpenny for a jam jar"

Some of the shops near us were hit by bombs but they mostly opened again soon. We didn't have to go far to get everything we needed. At the end of the road there was an oil shop, a fishmonger's, a grocer's and so on, and a shop where you could get money for old jam jars. You could get money for old rags and newspapers too.

I always had plenty to do at weekends, going round knocking on doors asking for jam jars. I did a paper-round as well to earn a bit of money, and I used to run errands for people in the street. I spent the money on the *Beano* mostly, but I couldn't afford it regularly. I went down to Ridley Road Market with my friends to look for orange boxes to use for firewood. Sometimes we'd break them up and sell them for sixpence a bundle. The boys that lived down Ridley Road thought it was their territory, so we might end up with just fish boxes, all wet they were. In some streets the kids were in gangs and they'd block one end of the street, so you couldn't get down.

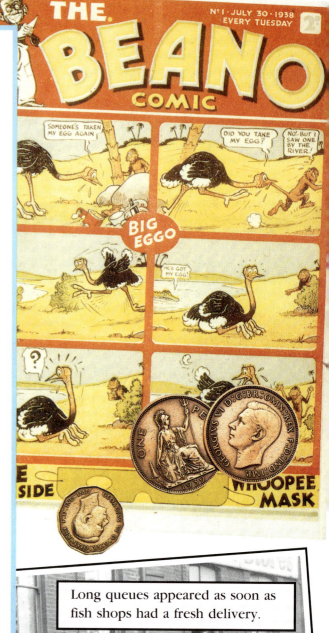

Long queues appeared as soon as fish shops had a fresh delivery.

2/6
2/11
EACH

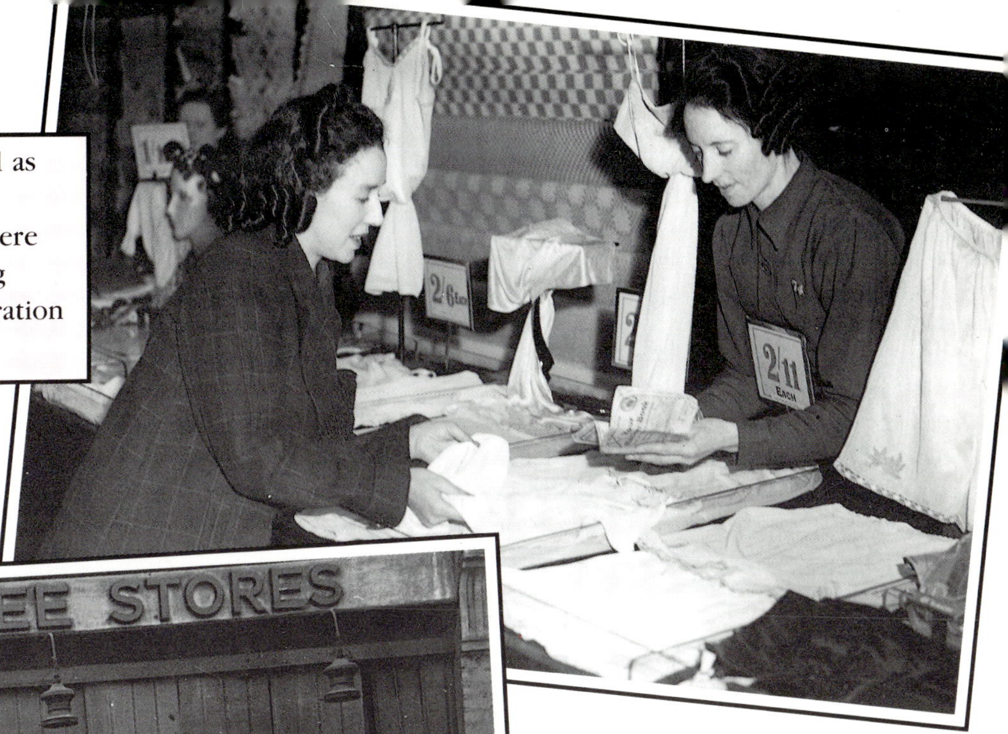

Clothes were rationed as well as food and the rules were very strict. Some shop assistants were even sent to prison for selling goods to customers without ration coupons.

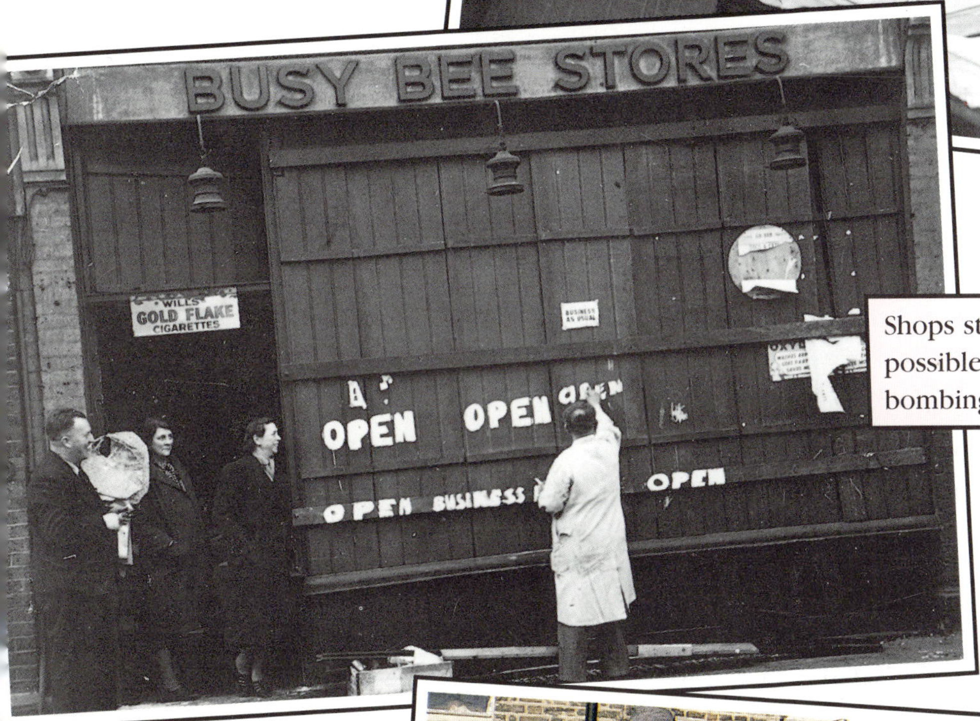

BUSY BEE STORES
WILLS
GOLD FLAKE
CIGARETTES
OPEN
OPEN
OPEN
OPEN
OPEN BUSINESS

Shops stayed open as much as possible even during the years of bombing raids.

THREE PENCE
1943
HALF PENNY
1937

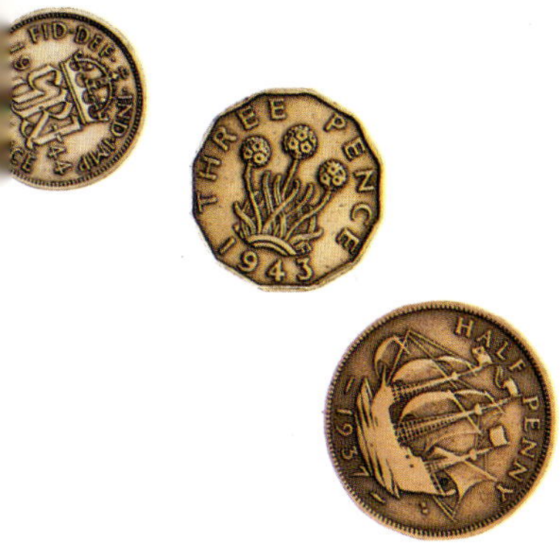

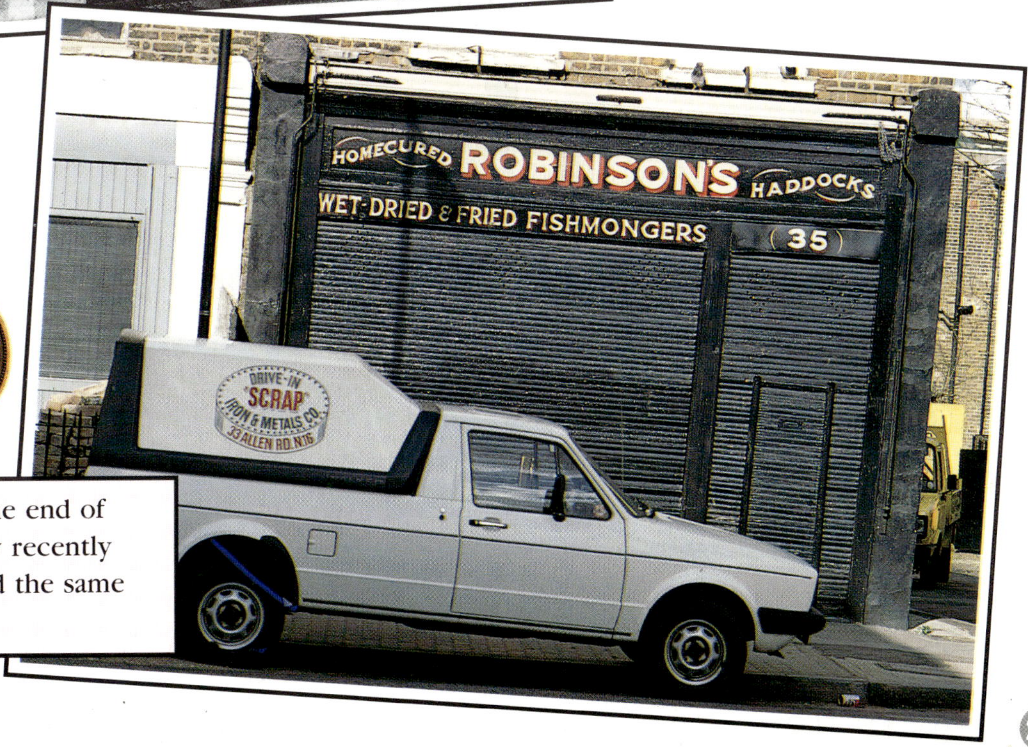

HOMECURED ROBINSON'S HADDOCKS
WET-DRIED & FRIED FISHMONGERS
35
DRIVE-IN
SCRAP
IRON & METALS CO.
33 ALLEN RD. N16

This fishmonger's at the end of Charlie's road has only recently closed down. It looked the same when he was a boy.

"A pennyworth of specks"

Nothing much got thrown away then. At school, if you had an apple, someone would always say, "Do you want the core?" and they'd be pleased to get it to eat. If you didn't want the skin another kid would always have it.

I used to buy a pennyworth of specks, apples with speckled skins. I couldn't afford to get proper apples. Sometimes I'd get a pennyworth of crackling from the fish shop, that was bits of batter. The grocer's sold broken biscuits or a pennyworth of cake crumbs.

Sweets were rationed, so if you ever saw an American soldier you always said, "Got any gum, chum?" They usually gave you some. I was on a bus in Oxford once and I asked an American GI for some gum. A woman said, "Oh, that's terrible, it's begging!", but in London it was normal.

America entered the war in 1941. G.I.s became a common sight in London.

When you could buy sweets, they came wrapped in a cone of newspaper like fish and chips did. You tore the newspaper in half afterwards to use in the lavatory.

We collected old cigarette cards. We played flicking games with them and we'd swap them. I collected army badges. My brother-in-law, Sid, was in the army in Algeria. He sent me a whole load of German badges in a kit-bag which didn't arrive, so I never got them. I was really upset.

H.M.S. "HOOD"

WILLS'S CIGARETTES

Shops damaged by bombing were quickly re-opened.

Cadets

Me in my St John's cadet uniform.

"Pretending to rescue people"

I was in the St John's Ambulance Brigade as a cadet from when I was eight till when I left school. The HQ was in the Mildmay Club on Newington Green, and when we were there we were "on duty". We used to march up and down in the back garden. We made sure we had smelling salts, dressings and bandages.

We met there every week and learnt how to salute and do First Aid. But if there had been an incident we wouldn't really have been allowed to do anything, we were too young. An unexploded shell landed on the green once. It blew out the window over the door which used to say St John's 47th.

Me and my friends used to run around with helmets on, pretending to rescue people. In the summer, I used to be out till very late and I'd forget the time. I didn't have a watch, and dad would be really cross when I got in.

I used to go on camps with the St John's. In fact, I was away on camp on the Isle of Sheppey when the war with Japan ended. We went down there on open-backed lorries. The journey was a bit rough.

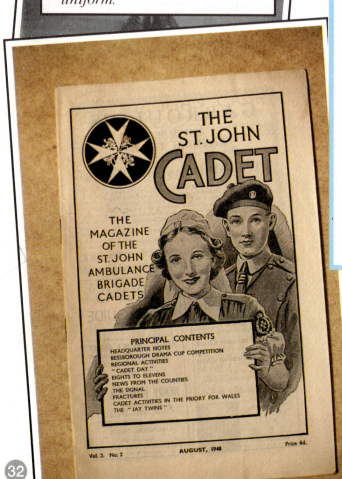

aily Mirror

MAY 2

Wednesday, May 2, 1945
12,906   ONE PENNY
Registered at G.P.O. as a Newspaper.

U-Boat chief claims he's new Fuehrer, tells Huns to fight on

HITLER DEAD

"Fell at his post in battle of Berlin," says Nazi radio

HITLER is dead. He "fell for Germany" in the Reich Chancellery in Berlin yesterday afternoon, according to a broadcast from Hamburg at 10.30 last night.

Grand-Admiral Doenitz, 54-year-old inventor of U-Boat pack tactics, broadcast, claiming that Hitler had appointed him Fuehrer and Commander-in-Chief of the German Forces.

Doenitz came to the microphone and declared: "The military struggle continues with the aim of saving the German people from Bolshevism.

"We shall continue to defend ourselves against the Anglo-Americans just as long as they impede our aim."

A ghost voice broke in: "Rise against Doenitz. The struggle is not worth while if crime wins."

Adolf Hitler, leader of the Nazi Reich since January 30, 1933, the world's chief criminal, now dead at the age of fifty-six. His career appears on Pages 4 and 5.

Admiral Doenitz.

The new "Fuehrer" for how long?

The announcement of Hitler's death at fifty-six, after being Fuehrer since January 30, 1933, was preceded by slow Wagnerian music and finally by a roll of drums.

During the announcement and Doenitz's speech from Hamburg, the southern German radio network went on broadcasting light music.

It was not until half an hour later that it put

Continued on Back Page

Doenitz lived here —in an asylum!

WHEN 50-year-old Admiral Karl Doenitz, Germany's new Fuehrer, invented the U-boat pack, his order to crews was: "Sink without mercy."

He left his job as U-boat chief to become C.-in-C. of the German Navy in February, 1943, and his technical brilliance was always a more formidable weapon than Hitler's intuition.

"The German Navy will fight to a finish," he has boasted.

During the last war he spent a considerable time in England—as a prisoner of war in a Manchester lunatic asylum.

The British sloop Snapdragon fished him out of the Mediterranean after sinking his U-boat in 1917.

By feigning insanity after his capture he qualified for a place among the first batch of prisoners to be repatriated to Germany.

He has shown himself capable of bluntly admitting the worst and fighting tenaciously in spite of it. Admitting in 1942 that U-boats had abandoned the deep Atlantic attacks off the American coast, he declared:

"Operating in American waters is no easy matter,

MYSTERY OF HIMMLER PUZZLES THE CABINET

By BILL GREIG

THE unexpected appearance of Admiral Doenitz as Fuehrer came as a shock to members of the Cabinet who have been in touch with the surrender discussions at all stages.

It had been assumed that Himmler would automatically succeed Hitler, and that this would be followed by complete surrender. What has gone wrong is not yet clear, but the belief is expressed officially that nothing has happened likely to lengthen the war appreciably.

The unknown factor is still Himmler. There are two possibilities.

That fanatical Nazis—of whom Doenitz is a fair specimen—and one of the toughest—have seized Himmler to prevent surrender.

That Doenitz, as leader, is nothing more than a screen behind which still another attempt to negotiate will be

made with Himmler holding the real power.

The possibility of Himmler also being dead was one which received some support last night, and the Government was making anxious attempts to find out the truth through neutral sources.

Despite his fighting speech Doenitz is not considered as really intending to stage a "fight to the last man" campaign. It is felt that behind his words lies no more than a desire to hearten the German people while he makes another effort . . . bound to be in vain . . . to get terms from the United Nations.

Doenitz and his friends may have believed that Himmler had succeeded in making a deal, safeguarding himself with

Britain and America. Regarding themselves double-crossed, they turned the tables on him.

That Himmler tried to save his own skin is now admitted.

It can now be revealed that it was Himmler and not Hitler who carried through all the arrangements regarding prisoners of war. He then gave the impression of being the real if not the titular head of Germany. At no time did Doenitz appear on the scene.

The possibility of Doenitz making some last desperate effort to hearten the Germans while he tries to negotiate is not overlooked here.

This might even include a renewal of air attacks on this country, but they could only be on a small scale.

The fact that the evacuation

of Norway and Denmark had apparently begun before Doenitz spoke suggests that Himmler had actually given some orders regarding surrender earlier in the day.

Attention is drawn to the fact that although Doenitz tried to suggest that Hitler died in action he carefully avoided saying so in as many words.

From one in close touch with the Government I was given this summing-up last night: "It is doubtful if whatever happened in Germany last night has lengthened the war by more than a week. The military position is as clear as that. Doenitz has no navy, no organised army and only the skeleton of an air force."

Victory

"The friendliness had gone"

At the end of the war, on VE day, there were big bonfires in the street and people brought out tables and chairs for a big party. I remember them burning figures of Hitler in Spenser Grove.

There was still rationing after the war ended and some things were difficult to get. I remember, in 1948, you couldn't get coal easily. I had to go a long way to get a 28lb sack and bring it home in the wheelbarrow.

We kept on the allotment for a bit, but the friendliness had gone. You'd go to pick your potatoes one day and they'd be gone. That hadn't happened in the war.

After nearly seven years of rationing people were prepared to wait in line to buy sweets.

Me and my wife-to-be in the
Victory Day party in my street.

The end of the war was
celebrated all over the country
with parties in the streets.

"A different film every night"

After the war we went to the Saturday morning cinema at the Ambassadors round the corner. You had a membership card, and on your birthday they gave you a free ticket. There were so many cinemas round us, you could go to a different film every night if you had the money. I went with mum to the pictures sometimes in the afternoon. She loved *Brief Encounter*. I liked the comedy films — Laurel and Hardy and Abbott and Costello.

It took a long time to rebuild all the streets round us and things seemed slow to get back to normal. Everyone in my family was working, so there was more money coming in. But there wasn't much to buy.

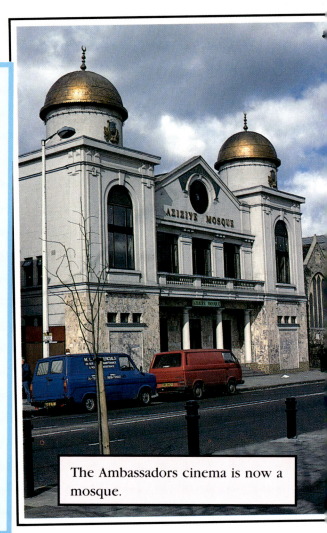

The Ambassadors cinema is now a mosque.

Shops on Stoke Newington Church Street just after the war.

The same buildings now.

At the end of the war, there were a lot of refugees came over from China. Some came to the China Inland Mission on Newington Green. They brought their sea-chests with them, but they had thrown away the keys on board ship so nobody could steal anything. My dad used to go and open the locks for them.

I came home from school at dinner time. Dad would be there since he worked from home. He cooked, but it wasn't very good. Dad used to go to the pub down the road. He played dominoes and cards. I don't think he gambled — or maybe he did, just for the next round of drinks.

Apprenticeship

"A poor and needy apprentice"

When I was fourteen, I went and got my first suit, so I could go for an interview to be an apprentice. I didn't wear it once I got the job, of course.

When I left school at fifteen, I was almost told what I was going to do. My mum had already decided I was going to be a plumber. She said, "Well, he'll never be out of work if he's a plumber." I don't think my dad had much say in it.

I never had any exams at school, no school certificate or anything. I started as an apprentice. I didn't earn much, about £1.13s a week. My friends were getting £2 or £3 doing labouring jobs. I used to think, "Oh well, it'll be all right later on."

CITY &

This is to
who satis

passed in
Examina

I won a prize at the end of my apprenticeship, that's me on the left.

LDS OF LONDON INSTITUTE

INCORPORATED BY ROYAL CHARTER

DOMINE DIRIGE NOS

DEPARTMENT OF TECHNOLOGY

that.................... CHARLES HENRY JONES

attended a Course of Instruction at.....................................

L.C.C. HACKNEY TECHNICAL COLLEGE

FIRST Class in the year 195 2 the INTERMEDIATE

PLUMBERS' WORK

Holbein.

Technology Committee

Directo...

P. McHugh.

Principal

Signat...

Me and my old plumbing tools.

I gave up a pound a week to my mum for my keep, and got a couple of bob a day back for my dinner money. I was apprenticed to a firm building houses in Hackney for the council.

I was lucky with my plumbing tools. There was a charity in Hackney that helped apprentices. If you could prove you were a poor and needy apprentice, they'd give you £20 to buy tools. That was a lot of money then. I went down to Tyzacks in Shoreditch to get myself set up and I've still got some of the tools now.

In the news

These are some of the important events which happened during Charlie's childhood.

1933 In the year Charlie was born, Adolf Hitler became Chancellor of Germany.

1936 The American athlete, Jesse Owens, won four gold medals at the Berlin Olympic Games. Hitler refused even to shake hands with him, because he was black.

1939 In September, Germany invaded Poland. Britain declared war on Germany three days later.

1940 In June, the German army captured Paris. A large part of the British army had to be rescued from the beaches of Dunkirk, in northern France. A fleet of warships and small vessels such as paddle-steamers, ferries, fishing-boats and pleasure-cruisers helped to transport the troops.

1940 In August, the German airforce began bombing British airfields, hoping to destroy the RAF (Royal Air Force). A few thousand young pilots, flying Hurricanes and Spitfires, fought against the German planes to win the Battle of Britain.

1940 In September, the blitz began, as the German airforce made regular bombing attacks on London and other major cities.

1941 In December, the Japanese launched a surprise attack on the American navy in Pearl Harbour, Hawaii. As a result, the USA declared war on Germany and Japan.

1945 In August, the first of two atomic bombs was dropped on Hiroshima, in Japan. Within a week, the Japanese surrendered and the war with them was over.

1944 In June, a huge army of Americans, Canadians, British and other allies landed on the beaches in Normandy, in northern France. This was known as the D-Day landings. It was 10 months before the Germans surrendered.

Things to do

Make a wartime scrapbook

Some of your relatives or neighbours may have memories of the Second World War. Their experiences may have been very different from those of Charlie Jones, particularly if they did not live in a big city. Show them this book and ask them how their wartime experiences compared.

If you have a cassette-recorder, you could tape their memories. Before you visit people, make a list of the subjects you want to talk about — for example, rationing, evacuation, school, bombing raids, etc. Some of the stories they tell you may be very sad, but some may well be funny. Ask your relatives and neighbours if they have any mementoes from the war that you could look at. Many people still have things like identity cards and ration books.

Go to your local library. Ask to see local wartime newspapers. Your library may have a local studies section. If so, ask the librarian if they have any photographs of your area from before the war. You probably will not find many actual wartime photographs, because very few were taken.

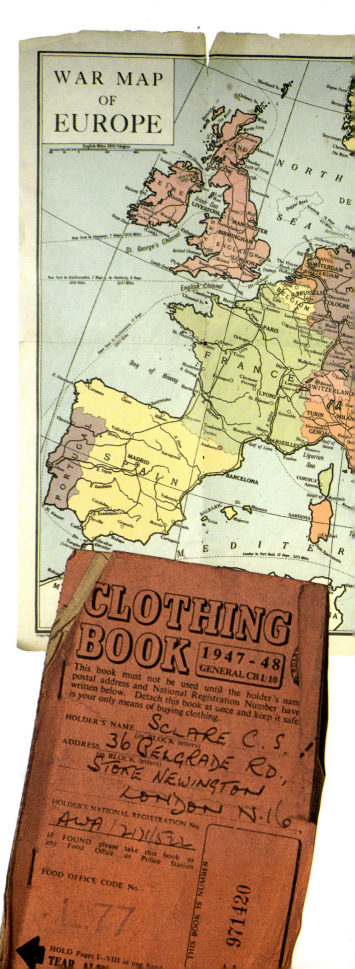

Look at a local map from fifty years ago and compare it with a modern one. See if you can find any differences in street names. Look for any buildings on the old map that may not be there any more, for example, any schools, factories or pubs.

Walk around your local area to see if there are any war memorials. Some buildings, for example, banks or libraries have wall plaques listing the names of servicemen who died in the war.

Use what you find out to make a scrapbook about the war.

Look at a modern map of Europe and compare it with this map of wartime Europe. What do you notice?

Find out if there is a local museum with any wartime exhibits. The Imperial War Museum in London is well worth a visit.

Glossary

Allotment
A small piece of land rented from the local Council on which vegetables can be grown.

Apprentice
Someone learning a trade. During the training, called an apprenticeship, the apprentice earns very little money.

ARP
Short for Air Raid Precautions, a government plan to reduce the damage and casualties caused by air raids. Civil Defence workers were responsible for air raids in their area and for enforcing ARP rules, such as the blackout.

Blitz
Short for *blitzkrieg*, a German word meaning lightning war. It is used mainly to describe the German bombing of British cities during the Second World War.

Coupons
Tickets issued by the government during the war, which had to be presented to a shopkeeper, when buying goods that were rationed. Only a certain number of food and clothing coupons were given to each person, every month.

Dig for Victory
A campaign launched by the government to encourage people to grow their own food.

Doodlebug
The nickname given to German V-2 flying bombs. These were pilotless rocket-powered aircraft packed with explosives. They made a very distinctive noise as they flew overhead. The noise suddenly stopped as the engine cut out and the doodlebug fell to the ground.

Evacuation
A policy introduced by the government at the start of the war to send children away from big cities, which were in danger of being bombed, to the safety of the countryside.

Gas mantle
A small cover put over the end of a gas jet to produce a light.

Kit-bag
A long, thin cylindrical canvas bag in which members of the armed forces packed their clothes and personal possessions.

Mission
A charity which looks after people in need.

Oilcloth
A type of cloth treated with oil to make it waterproof. It was once used as a floor covering in kitchens and bathrooms.

Raid
An air raid by enemy bombers.

Rationing
A system for sharing out goods in short supply, usually by using coupons. Rationing was needed in the Second World War, because so many ships bringing supplies from abroad were sunk by German submarines.

Siren
A machine which produced a loud wailing note to warn people that an air raid was about to start. A siren also sounded the 'all-clear' when the raid was over.

Smelling salts
Salts with an extremely powerful smell. They are held under the nose of someone who has fainted to help them recover consciousness.

Trolleybus
A bus powered by overhead cables. The electricity is picked up by two long metal rods which stick up from the roof of the trolleybus.

Index

HITLER'S EMPIRE, SPLIT IN TWO, MAKES ITS LAST STRUGGLE
Allies from East and West unite, then turn to deliver the final blows

THIRD REICH IS DEAD

At 4 p.m., April 25, in its 13th year

HANDSHAKE ON TWISTED GIRDER LINKS ARMIES

From SELKIRK PANTON: Torgau on the Elbe, Friday

THE Third Reich of Adolf Hitler is dead. It died in its 13th year at four o'clock on Wednesday afternoon, when General Courtney Hodges' First U.S. Army linked up with Marshal Koniev's First Ukrainian Army and cut Germany into two parts, north and south.

Two junior officers—Lieutenant William Robertson, of California, and Lieutenant Alexander Silvachko, the Russian, shook hands on a twisted girder of the wrecked Torgau railway bridge over the Elbe and arranged details for the meetings between the regimental and divisional commanders on both sides, which took place yesterday.

Soon, Hodges and Koniev will meet.

Torgau, which nearly 200 years ago saw the victory of Frederick the Great's Prussians over the Austrians, saw history made again while its shell-wrecked buildings burned in the fresh spring breeze and smoke overhung the town.

WINE, SONG AND MUSIC

Now the Russians—Rooskies as the Americans call them affectionately—are celebrating the momentous link-up with wine, song and music.

The wine, drunk in beer mugs, comes from the cellars of Torgau, and the music from the piano accordions "liberated" from the Wehrmacht storehouse in the almost deserted town.

I was one of three British journalists who were present at the headquarters of the 273rd Infantry Regiment, 69th Division, of General Hodges' Army when the first flash came in to say the link-up had been made.

We had just walked into the regimental command, in a palatial manor house behind the lines, when the radio operator shot into the room and cried: "I think we've contacted the Russians."

In an instant the headquarters sprang into action. Colonel C. M. Adams, the commander of the regiment, took the message. It ran: "Mission accomplished; making arrangements for meeting G.I.s; no casualties."

The flash came from Lieutenant Albert Kotzebue, of Texas, who had been sent out on patrol eastwards towards the Russians. The time was 3.20 p.m. He was told to stay put and await further instructions.

But his friend, Lieutenant William D. Robertson, of Los Angeles, of the same 273rd Regiment, had better luck. He went out on patrol and never thought that he should have done. And he met the Russians.

This is the story he told me: "I guess I must have gone too far. There were floods of people streaming back towards Wurzen, and German soldiers and officers were throwing away arms as my 20 men from our jeeps kept going along.

"I figured I could not stop to disarm these Jerries, so I kept going until suddenly I was in Torgau, and there were the Rooskies on the other side of the Elbe.

FLAG ON CASTLE TOWER

"I heard some firing, small arms stuff, so I got some white cloth and paint from a wrecked drug store and made a kind of Stars and Stripes.

"I went up on a tower of the old castle overlooking the river and waved the flag. They stopped firing. I shouted 'Tovarish (comrade), kamerad.'

"They fired flares. I shouted I did not have flares, but they could not hear. They started firing again. It turned out that they had been fooled only the day before by Germans with a home-made American flag.

"So I left the flag flying and started out on the wrecked bridge, climbing over the debris. At the same time a Russian armoured car came down their end of the bridge and a soldier started crawling towards me. When we came together we kind of said 'Hello' and shook hands. We exchanged watches as mementoes."

Robertson then went across to the east side of the Elbe and met a Russian major and other officers. "We had a bottle of wine, a can of sardines, chocolates, and some biscuits. We drank a lot of toasts, and they filled my water-bottle with schnapps."

'THE RUSSIANS ARE HERE!'

On Wednesday night, as we were in quarters waiting news from the American front line, we were alarmed just before midnight and told: "The Russians are here at headquarters."

We raced down in the moonlight to divisional headquarters, and there followed one of the strangest Press conferences ever held—a mixture of news, wine, cognac, vodka, speeches, and interviews with the young American and Russian officers who made the first contact. In the room of General Emil Reinhardt, C.O. 68th Infantry Division, more than 40 war correspondents, a dozen U.S. officers and four Russian officers crammed

► BACK PAGE, COL. FOUR

Panton was a prisoner

REPORTING the historic link-up is the climax of an extraordinary career for SELKIRK PANTON.

Chief correspondent in Berlin for the Daily Express until the war, Panton was captured by the Germans in Denmark and was repatriated two months ago.

After four weeks in London he was assigned to cover the U.S. First Army. And now on his journey back to Berlin he is the man on the spot for the cutting of Germany into two.

TWO ARMIES MOVE TO PINCER MUNICH

From MONTAGUE LACEY

SUPREME H.Q., Friday.—With the Allied link-up, vast forces have been released to turn to the destruction of the two pockets of Hitler's empire in north and south.

In the south American tanks crashed into the fortress of Austria.

The German First Army is reeling under the blows of both General Patch's Seventh Army and Patton's Third Army, sweeping down on Munich and the Austrian Alps.

German defences have been broken in many places. We are 25 miles from Munich and 70 from Salzburg, now reported to be the seat of the German Government.

The Third Army crossed the Adriatic frontier two miles south of the junction with the Czech and German frontiers.

The 86th Division has captured Ingolstadt, on the Danube, and is astride the Munich-Nuremberg motor road, with the enemy showing little fight.

Two great steel pincers are closing now around Munich as the Third and Seventh Armies race to encircle the largest German city in the south.

GENOA IS CAPTURED, NEARING VENICE

From JAMES COOPER

ITALY, Friday Night.—Genoa, the most important port in Italy, was entered today by an American task force.

The way to the birthplace of Christopher Columbus was made for them by patriots, who had already captured a large part of the city and opened the way for the Americans and American-Japanese under Major-General Almond.

There is no report yet on what Marshal and his wife were given ordinary prison food. In fact their breakfast of bread and butter and asked for beef tea instead of coffee. But most of the food was still on the tray when it was handed out. For lunch they asked for an omelette.

Commenting on this, the Left Radical Franc-tireur writes: "All it confirmed, this statement is a pure scandal. We expect a denial or an explanation."

Mme Marcelle Belle, who jumped on a chair as a Socialist oration in Spandau last night and spoke in favour of Petain, was arrested.

RED ARMY SEIZES BERLIN AIRFIELD

STALIN officially confirmed the last night the capture of Spandau, north-west Berlin suburb which gives its name to the Spandau machine gun, and Potsdam.

The Russians also took the Tempelhof airfield, in southeast Berlin. More than 11,500 of Berlin's defenders went into the prisoner cages. Eighty-five planes were captured.

Soviet troops have also advanced 45 miles west of Berlin.

In the north fresh advances are squeezing the Baltic pockets. The Russians swept 30 miles west of the Elbe at Stettin to take Prenslau.

GERMANS FLEE EMDEN IN U BOATS

CANADIAN ARMY, Friday.—Fifty German submarines—500 and 250 tonners—have arrived at Emden during the past few days, and are believed to be setting up a shuttle service taking troops to Denmark or Norway. Considerable area traffic has been seen around the Frisian Islands, whose big coastal guns have been trained on the Canadians.—B.U.P.

Won't-surrender general seized

BREMEN, Friday.—Captured at Bremen today were General Becker, the commander who refused to surrender the city; Major-General Weiner Siber, garrison commander; and in the port a vice-admiral with 10 U boats and a destroyer.—Reuter News Service.

'THE YANKS ARE HERE'—'THE RUSSIANS ARE HERE'

INFANTRYMEN of the U.S. First Army have worked their way across a broken bridge over the Elbe, and extend their hands to grasp the welcoming hands of Russian neighbours. . . There was singing and dancing on the east bank of the river afterwards, much slapping-on-the-back between Americans and Russians and many toasts in the sunshine.

Petain sleeps by death post

From ROBIN DUFF: Paris, Friday

MARSHAL PETAIN and his wife slept tonight, in two low, narrow, oak bedsteads on the ground floor of the Fort Montrouge, south of Paris.

Their room, bare except for essentials, measures 13ft. by 10, and its window is iron-barred.

Outside in the post at which traitors condemned since the liberation of Paris have been shot.

To enter the Marshal's prison you must pass through another, which is even smaller. In that room are two posts which are used every day. No-one may enter in permanent attendance on Petain. Two Army doctors, a captain and a lieutenant are on call.

In the passage outside their room in the fort, Paris gendarmes march slowly up and down. One hundred are on guard duty.

The State Prosecutor, M. André Mornet, has said of Petain: "His strong arm of France before Reynaud in March 1940. He was Prime Minister in 1933 when Hitler came to power, and was one of the signatories of the Munich Agreement in 1938. He is 61."

REDOUBT A MYTH SAYS DIETMAR

'When Berlin goes, all is over': Hitler is there'

Express War Reporter: Germany, Friday

GENERAL KURT DIETMAR, German High Command radio spokesman, has surrendered. He told his American captors in the Magdeburg sector that Hitler is still in Berlin, and will die there; that the Redoubt is a myth, and that the war will end within a few days.

Dietmar crossed the Elbe in a rowing-boat on Wednesday, and walked into the American lines on the Ninth Army front, accompanied by his 16-year-old son Bernhardt and his aide-de-camp, Major Werner Pluskat.

He was asked if he wished to give himself up and was given half an hour to decide.

Within a few minutes he had made his choice: "I will be safer with you," he said. "I surrender."

Dietmar told American officers "Hitler is still in Berlin. But Berlin will fall, and Hitler will either be killed or will capitulate. Then the war will end in a few days.

"One of three generals—soon Braunbausch, Guderian or von Rundstedt—will take control, and will make peace immediately on almost any terms."

"The Redoubt is a myth. When Berlin falls it will be all over."

"Goering has probably been executed already."

'The man who knew'

Daily Express Radio Editor, G. W. Frerk, writes:

DIETMAR, who always knew what was coming, was the most plausible among Nazi radio spokesmen. His regular Tuesday war commentaries on the German home radio had a nation-wide audience.

For a song-time Dietmar was believed to be just a "voice" invented by Goebbels, until in summer 1943 the Germans provided a few b-ograph [sic] to prove that he was a real, live general.

He is 57, and commanded a battalion in the last war. When that war broke out he was commander of the Military Engineers' School in Berlin. He took part in the invasion of Norway, and in 1941 became radio spokesman for the German High Command.

Cancellations of his announcements were usually an indication of important developments. With the arrival of the Allied armies on German soil his absence became more frequent.

He made his last personal appearance on March 15, when he said: "We have been pressed back to our last inner defence ring of the fortress Germany. The command of the hour is that we must fight hard for what is left."

This station is closing down...

General Kurt Dietmar, the Wehrmacht radio commentator, lips tightly clamped together, is driven away in a jeep after crossing the Elbe to make his surrender.

Himmler men shoot Goering

SAYS GERMAN

ZURICH, Friday.—A German diplomat from Munich revealed today the background to Goering's "resignation."

He said: "Last Monday Goering sent Hitler an urgent

4 a.m. LATEST

HITLER CALLS TO BERLIN WOMEN

Hamburg radio says Hitler has issued new appeal to all women and girls to take up arms to fight the Russians.

---

letter asking him, with the Nazi Party, to accept the consequences of a lost war and prevent the further shedding of German blood.

"The same night Himmler sent his own bodyguard to Goering's home, and Goering's fate was sealed. His wife, Emmy, was present."

"One report says that Goering was ordered to the commandant of Himmler's bodyguard who his own death sentence whereupon he first shot his two daughters and then himself."

"Another version is that the bodyguard mowed down Goering and his wife without warning.—Exchange

---

Mussolini is held: wife turned back

From FREDERICK GLEANER

BERNE, Friday.—It is reported from inside Italy tonight that Mussolini has been captured by partisans at Nesso, on Lake Como, just south of the Swiss frontier.

Arrested with him are Graziani, his C-in-C, Guido, his Minister of the Interior, Parinacci, former secretary of the Fascist Party, and Pavolini, secretary-general of the Republican Fascist Party.

One version of the capture is that the partisans surprised Mussolini and his henchmen at lunch.

They intended to try escaping into Switzerland by way of Chiasso.

It is known that Mussolini's wife, Donna Rachele, has already tried to get over the frontier.

She and her daughter asked at Chiasso for permission to enter Switzerland.

While Donna Rachele pleaded with the frontier guards, eight small cars loaded with their dark, keeping well out of reach.

The head of the front-er post told Donna Rachele he had instructions from the Federal Council they could not enter. The cars turned back into Italy.

Italy is likely to claim the right to try Mussolini instead of sending him to an international court as a war criminal.

Victory prizes for young composers

THE Daily Express announces today a Victory Music Contest, open to young British composers.

Two prizes are offered—one of £250, the second £150.

The contest is sponsored by the Daily Express to herald the approach of victory and peace.

And it is in the spirit of those composers should find their inspiration.

The contest is for a symphonic work of one or more movements, fully orchestrated, playing time between 15 and 20 minutes.

It is open to British composers. Entries must reach the Daily Express not later than October 31, 1945, accompanied only by the name and address of the composer, but also by a nom de plume.

Noms de plume only will accompany the scores when they are placed for adjudication before—

Mr. Arthur Bliss,
Mr. Malcolm Sargent, and
Mr. Constant Lambert,

who have agreed to act as judges.

A public performance of the prize-winning works under the baton of a well-known conductor will be arranged at the Albert Hall next winter by the Daily Express.

The Daily Express also undertakes to bring to the attention of leading conductors the six best compositions which do not win a prize.

Reynaud and Daladier free

TWO former French Premiers and the man who was Allied Commander-in-Chief before the German march on Paris have crossed from Germany into Switzerland, said Paris radio last night. They are:—

PAUL REYNAUD, the Premier of France to whom Mr. Churchill suggested an Anglo-French union in June 1940.

Reynaud favoured the plan, but the French Cabinet rejected it. He tried to reach Spain by car, but was badly hurt in a crash. He is 67.

GENERAL MARIE GUSTAVE GAMELIN, C-in-C of the Allied Armies in 1939, who placed his faith in the Maginot Line. He is 73.

EDOUARD DALADIER—known as "the strong man of France" until superseded as Premier by Reynaud in March 1940. He was 59.

Two other former French Premiers, M. Blum and M. Herriot, are near St. Mancaeren on the German-Bavaria border.

The Germans are to release all Allied civilian internees, the French Minister for Prisoners confirms.

Nazis worry about their poison gas

NEAR REGENSBURG, Friday.—Germans in Regensburg had huge stores of poison gas but they made no attempt to use them, said positions to the Americans so that it could be safely removed.—A.P.

Missed—the 12.15

THIRD ARMY, Friday.—Knaudling's private 35-car train has been captured 20 miles from Regensburg.

Dried egg ration halved

The dried egg ration will be cut from two packs to one a month from tomorrow until May 26, says the Food Ministry.

Improving

Britain: Dry, cold, showery overnight, improving.

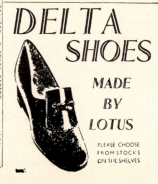
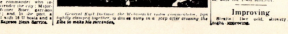